The Romantic Chronicles Of a Manic Depressive

By: Emily Ann Carroo

Prologue:

I make art for myself. I'm not here to sugarcoat or be precious. Everything I write is rooted in real life or inspired by something real. Art has a perspective, and mine is raw, unedited, and unapologetic. I'm not trying to avoid stepping on toes or to protect your feelings.

If my art made you feel anything at all, then it did its damn job.

New York
for the taking

It was never as it seemed,
Yet it was always home to me.
The clacking of my heels, step by step,
On the pavement created a rhythm—
A sway in my hips, a swing in my hair,
As it danced around my shoulders.

The city noise became my orchestra.
I paraded myself through the streets,
Silk draped on my long, slender legs.
Delusion and intoxication—
The streets glittered,
Creating a sense of inspiration.

New York City, as a young girl,
Will always looks real pretty.
New York City was always mine
For the taking.

Innocent till proven puberty

I remember life before sex.
I remember the innocence.
Puberty came too late.
Suddenly, you have tits—
So you get free coffee.

It never truly occurred to me
Until someone forced me into
Feeling.

Feeling like—I am a woman.
And I'm not sure
I like the power in this feeling.
I was so young,
So naïve,
To actually think
It couldn't happen to me.

I pushed it down,
Eventually forgot—
Until something stupid
Came along.

Like the ticking of the clock,
Metronome,
Back and forth.
Watch the big hand chasing,
Tightening round my neck.
A gasp for air,

The swoosh of wind
Through my hair.

Time pauses, and all you
Feel is this womanly body.
That's why they stare.
What makes me
Uneasy:
The lack of control
Of men in society.

Dressed up to feel sexy,
Stripped down to skin to feel seen.
The rise of my thigh,
Their eyes travel all around me,
Inspecting me,
Like I'm their trophy.

TAKE ME.
IT'S FREE.

I can't believe there was
Life before sex.
Sex is violence.
Sex sets you free.
Without any sexy,
There'd be no me.

Puberty changes everything.

Flower
Child

The sun danced across her skin—
Over her breast,
Around her neck,
Up to her chin.

A twinkle in her eyelashes,
Embracing the day.

Sparkles in the sun's rays,
Bending and weaving through
Daydreams
That twirl in the air.

A goddess, she dances—
Sunshine
In her hair.

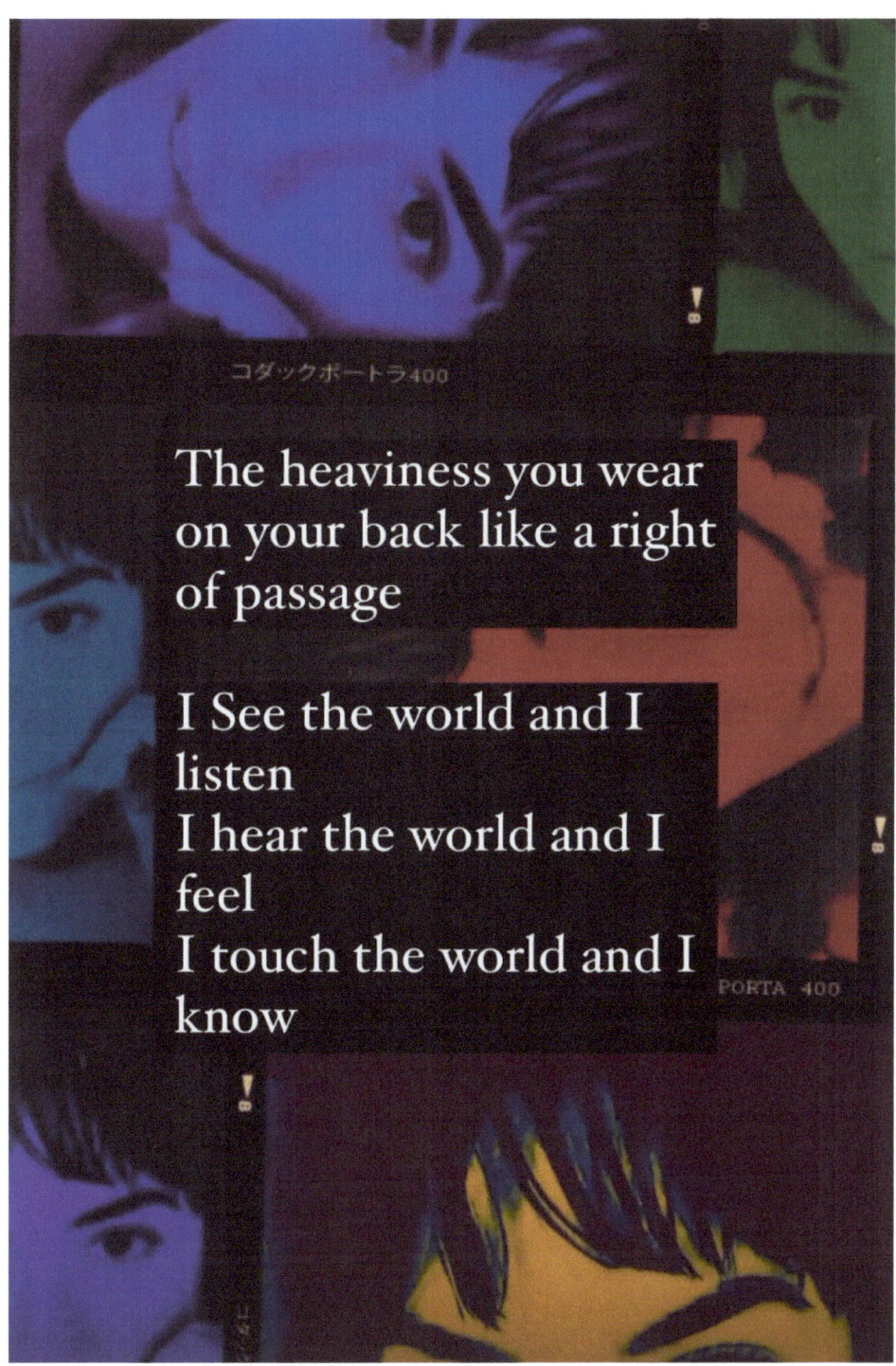

The heaviness you wear
on your back like a right
of passage

I See the world and I
listen
I hear the world and I
feel
I touch the world and I
know

Your inspiration

Of course,
I inspired your next art piece.
There's shit that goes on inside me.
I'm not vapid or empty—
Not like the endless checklist of women
You usually
Exchange spit with.

I'm a muse,
With the curse of being
Everyone else's lesson.
Easy to love,
And easy to lose.

The lover of a lifetime,
But the reason for your
Downfall, too.

We are all prostitutes at the end of the day.

Some of us just don't learn our worth,
So we live a life of delusion.

Tell me—who do you sell your body to
When you play dress-up?
If not for yourself,
Then who are you trying to impress?

Whores just make you pay for their time.
What's the crime in that—
If not jealousy for being magnetic?

My presence isn't cheap, and neither is my time.

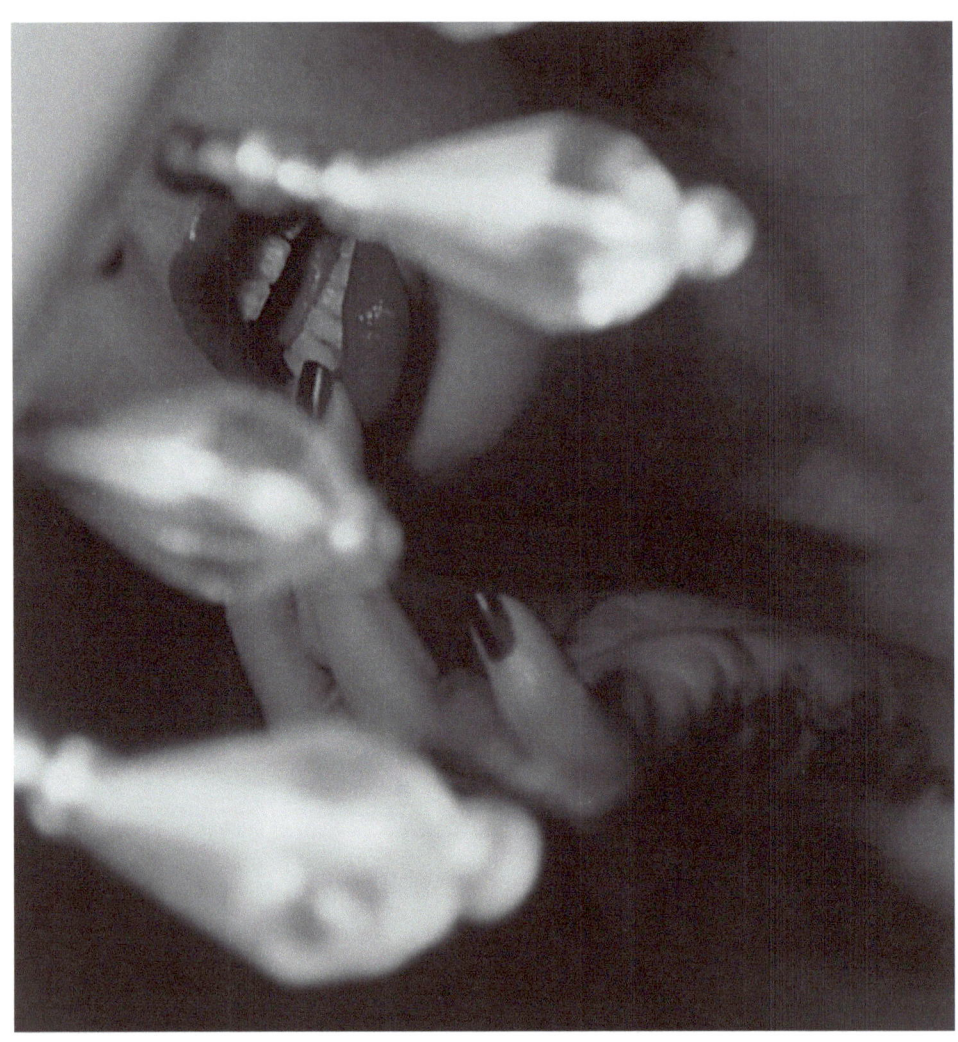

I want to love a painter.
"Draw me like one of your French girls."

I want to feel his heart
Throbbing inside me.

I want to love a painter,
So he can pour me into a colorful world
With every stroke.

I go weak.
I want to love a painter—
Give him something to

Eat.

Heal.

You can let it affect you forever,
Or you can acknowledge that it happened—
Allow yourself to heal
And grow from it.

You don't have to forget,
But why carry the weight
Of a hundred stones
Every day for the rest of your life—
Stones that weren't even placed there by you?

You'd have back pain forever.

I ~~hate~~ you.

I hate you.
I didn't think I was capable, but
I hate you.

You've done more damage than good—
More of a pain in my ass,
And that's the polite way to say
Cancer.

But I hate you.
You were good,
Then you weren't.

Too old,
Too jaded,
A junkie that kinda made it,
But left a tornado wherever
You went.

"I hate you"
Is just where it begins.

I don't wish you ill—
I just don't care.
I don't curse your name—
I just don't fucking care,
As if I never even knew your
Name.

I hate you,

And that's just it.
You had me convinced
You were all,
And we were it.
That's it.

Right now,
Don't feel like
Messing around.
Am I just too cool for ya?
What's going down?

On the edge of my tongue,
There's a taste of your lips—
But the sting that it brings…

Why'd you have to taste so

Sweet?

I prefer
Savoury things.

Pearls.

Drape me in pearls,
Let them drag across my skin—
Slowly.
Around my breasts,
Between my legs,
With every bump,
I lose my breath.

Build me up
Until the pearls could
Nearly strangle me.
Tie my wrists—
But with jewels, with pearls,

In pearls,
Please.

Dont love me

It always happens,
It happens to me.
I fall in love,
I fall apart,
Forget how to be me.

Get lost in a man,
Let him under my skin,
Into my veins—
He becomes a cancer in me.

By the time I learn
What it's doing to me,
I start to fight back,
And they start to beat me.

I'm a bitch with my words,
A thief with their hearts.

When will I learn,
That in love,
Love will set you free?

So you see,
It ain't so easy.
And I know
It seems so deceiving.

I'm only good to love
When you're not
In love with me.

NYC city of dreams

Central Park in the summer—
The city's heart center.

People being people,
So many lives just living, passing by.
A million faces—
I wonder what they're thinking.

This is life,
This is all that's been turning.
The sexual tension in the heat,
A city of strangers.

A hundred brand-new faces,
And out of all the places
In the world,
There's nowhere
I'd rather be
Than in New York City.

Mr.Sadness

Mr. Sadness crept into my mind,
Dumped himself in the pages of my memory.
He chased me down a tunnel
Lit with colors I'd never seen—
Stealing a kiss laced with desire,
Biting down on my lip.

Voices whispered with his breath,
Hissing down my neck,
Seducing me with his box of edges,
Luring me into his fantasy.

Mr. Sad Man,
Why won't you let me be?
If you want a grave,
Let's dig a hole.

Running, panting,
Out of breath—
Without a trace.

Mr. Sadness danced around the room,
All over the place,
Inside me, between me.

Mr. Sadness,
I want to feel nothing, too.

<u>Not</u> Your Muse

You say "Muse,"
And I feel raped.
Consumed, sucked
Dry.

Performative.
Precious.

Men say "Muse,"
And it
Fills me
With hate.

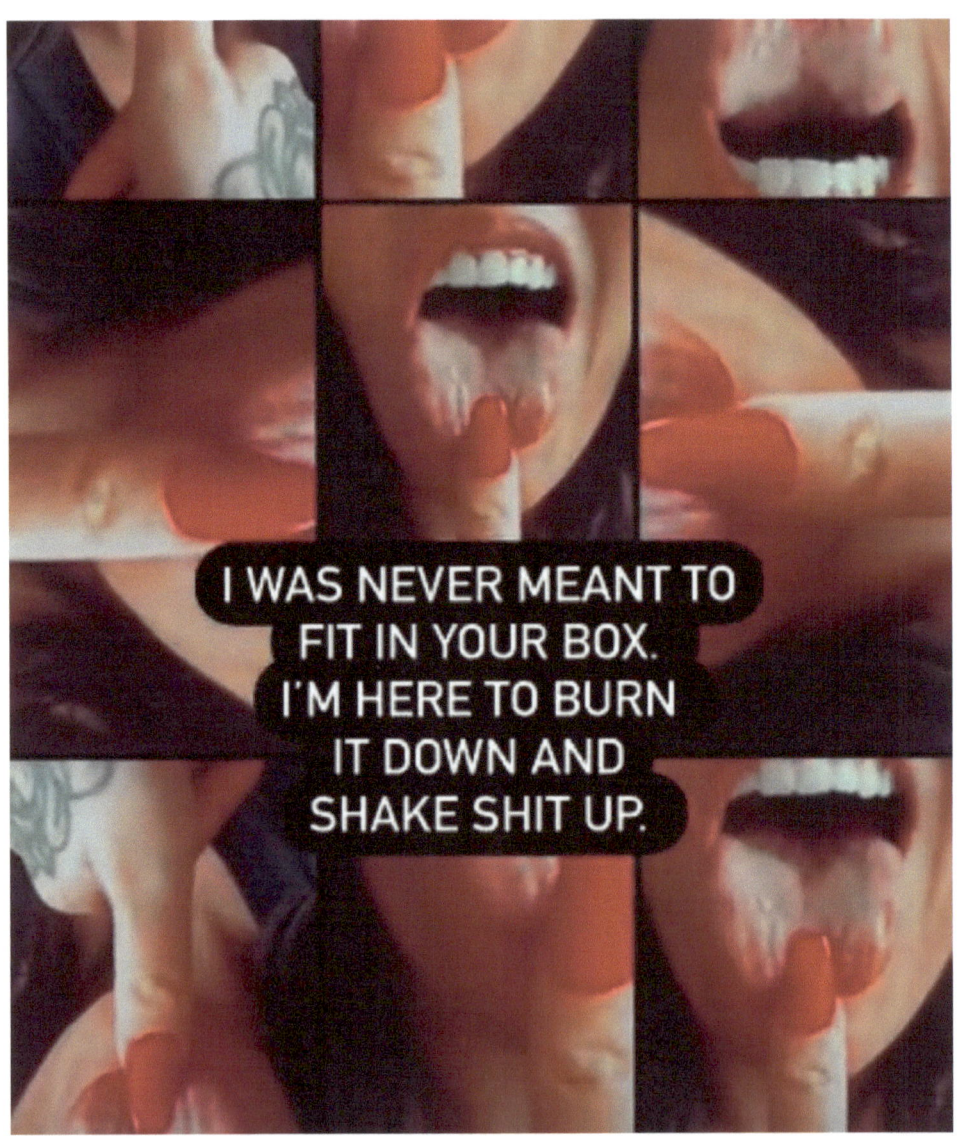

Devour me. See me

Take your tongue,
Drag it from my hip bone.
Let it glisten over my stomach—
Stop for a beat.

Capture me with your eyes.
Kiss me.
Kiss again… right here.
Stare into me.

Dance your fingers up my silks,
Watch my skin jump.
Hear my breath whistle.

Bite into something sweet.
Feast on my skin,
Suckle the juices—
Dripping in luxury,
Roses and marijuana smoke.

Lower your eyes,
Look up and see me—
The view of an addictive palate.

Quiver.
I'm watching you,
Watch me too.
Excited, watching you squirm—
Thinking I won't make you melt.
Completely seduce you.

Devour me
Before I destroy you.
Smoke me in.
Exhale my perfume.

Sip on my red stain,
Blood drawn from my
Cherry pain.
Drink me up in the morning,
Make me gasp at the sound of
You.

Lick your fingers dry,
Leaning into kind-of wanting you.
So take me in.
Watch me sparkle in the afternoon.

Come on, it can't be that easy.

Do you fall in love so easily?
Or are you just discovering the
Magic of a woman—
Beauty
That beams with authenticity?

See me.

More cocaine please.

The cocaine wasn't as addictive as you.
You sit and watch me—

Growing every second.
You don't think
                    I see.

                    How do you feel?
I can see how badly
You want me.

Brown leather and champagne
Down my throat,
You fill up my senses

With something delicious.

Drip.
Drop.
Good times.

Champagne on the ceiling.

Seasons of Lust.

I remember November—
When you wore that striped sweater.
You held me down,
And we kissed for the first time,
Crossing on Grand Street.

You met me in the city.
I picked out the leather just for you.
I wanted to be your rock 'n' roll queen,
Wanted to make all your fantasies true.

You fell apart in the bedroom;
I held you in the bathroom.
One more line, and I'd be with you—
Soho Grand, queen suite dreams.

I fell for you the first night you made me cry,
Holding my hand in the taxi.

Can you ever forgive me?
I never knew my worth,
But I found it
Loving you.

I remember December—
I wrote my heart in a letter.
You came back,
Said you'd never let me go.

Where do I go?
How did I let it go so wrong?

When the money you make
Is the price that you pay,
There's no love for ladies of lust.

I need you.
I don't want you.
I need the man—
The only man meant for me.

But I burned his feet,
And he's been running,
So damn far away from me.

The winter froze over my mind—
With images of you.
It stung my lungs,
Inhaling all of you.

High on the idea of what we could be.

I get high to get naked
and learn to love myself.

Feline Ecstacy

You say you want to make me quiver,
Yet I'm a queen in the throes
Of ecstasy.

I flourish in the flames,
Draw you in with my dance.
Sex is my spell,
And you've been put in a trance.

Vulnerability—my weakness.
Strike when hot,
Strike when true.
But don't dare try to seduce me
When I'm enchanted too.

Trickle on my fingers,
Steal a kiss for admission.
Haunting your memories
With a love affair
That never came true.

I'm not your baby girl.
I don't even want you.
I just want a drink
And a place to stay—
Till I no longer need to.

Hollywood can suck my D**K

Surrounded and completely alone.
Together—but it's just you.
In a city of big lights,
Everything seems possible—
Until the "Big Man" says,
"You're just a woman.
Now sit down.
Show me your talents."

Hollywood catastrophe.

Take me now.
Lose some weight.
Change my hair.
Then you'll have me.

Playing dumb, playing pretend.
I'm so hungry
For drugs they won't feed me.

I just wanna be old Hollywood dreamy—
Not this bullshit:
I'm a damsel in distress.
Please come and save me!

Punk chic that talks back,
Questions you too—
With hips and tits,
Middle fingers to society.

Hollywood breakdown
For the broken and the true.
Hollywood catastrophe,
I once believed in you.

Ew.

Master Manipulator

Wait.

Don't come any closer—
I think I might kill you.
I can still smell her perfume.

Take three steps back,
Turn around,
Open that door.
Get the fuck out.

You make leaving you so easy.
But you still wanna see me?
You say we could still be friends?

The friends I know
Don't treat me like you.
You say you care about me too—
Say that I'm crazy?
Yeah, that's true, baby,
But so are you.

You make it so damn easy—
So fucking easy to leave you.

Take one more step,
And I'll lose my cool.
I don't wanna go to jail,
But you're acting a fool.

Enough with the names,
Enough with the blame game.
You're just a sad, miserable—
I don't owe you shit.

I don't owe you my body.
You convinced me,
Thinking you'd marry me.
When you put on the ring,
I froze. I tapped out.

Yeah, I know that hurt you.
I tried to be there too—
More than I ever got from you.

Won't answer your calls.
Trash took itself out.
You're just one less thing
I have to worry about.

I'm not sorry that you're leaving.
I cried enough to fill the world.
I hope you choke on your tears.
I hope it hurts to know.

You think you're so cool—
Think you're this sweet, kind man.
Tell me,
What kind of man paints his girl
With his fists?
Pretends to be someone new
For everyone else—
But I know the truth.

Toxic love.
Toxic waste.
I'm getting myself out of this place.

If I don't,
Then I know—
I'm bound to explode.

I'm letting go.
I'll pack up your suits.
Running to get out.

You're always starting these mind games,
Then tell me I'm the "only one for you."
You make leaving you so easy.

You'll look back and realize—
I was the one
Who figured out all your
Twisted heart's torture.

You thought you'd change me,
But I got better.

You left me,
Ran back to her,
Then came crawling to me
Because she wouldn't kiss you?

Wait.
You must think
I'm dumb or something.

Staring back at me.

I get stuck in the mirror,
Stuck in the heart of my eye—
Like my subconscious
Is trying to warn me.

But I come back,
Over and over,
Looking for answers.

As if,
If I stare long enough—
Deep enough—
I'll see it.

A box full of heroin,
Feelin' thin,
Addicted to a deadly sin.

The drug?
It's not what I'm interested in.
I want the feeling,
Not the high.

I want the roller coaster—
Mucky waters,
Janky, jagged edges.

Me?
I'm not afraid of needles,
But I don't buy
What you're selling.

When the drugs don't work,
Do more drugs.
(Don't actually do more.)

Go manic.

Fall in love with making men fall in love with you.

We are mindfully mindless
To each other, all the time.

Good intentions—
And bruised egos.

~~Blinded~~ Love

Dancin in the Dark

I've been walking heartbroken—
Step by step for a while now.
A dream isn't something you capture;
It's something you reach for,
Chase over and over,
Until you can taste it on your lips.

I wanna love you,
But I wanna run away.

I wanna hold you,
But I want to feel like I'm not

Missing my shot at seeing the world.

I fall in love
In all the wrong places,
At all the wrong times.
I'm the best lover you'll ever have—
But
only for one night.

I can't get too close.
I run when you get in.

If you're lucky,
You won't stay—
A lost cause in the wrecking.

Waiting for an opening,
A moment of clarity—
That I finally see

There's more to me than my body.

What's done in the dark
Is seen in the light.

Dancing in the night,
Dancing in the dark.

I apologize—
My emotions are high.
I can't feel my fingers.
I shouldn't be near you right now.

I'm tired of trying
To hold on to you,
Slipping away
In my own head.

But I know,
By the end of the night,
I'll be biting your lip,
Riding on your insecurities
That eat your heart out.

Lets Order take out.

Feed my ego.

The problem is,
I become the drug.
I sweep them up in a romance,

And I will be silent—
Take my clothes off on rooftops.

Drag your fingertips,
Lightly brushing my breast,
The tingling of cold air—
Your lips on my neck,
Gasping on rooftops.

Dancing in daydreams,
Lingerie lunch breaks,
Midnight feastings.

I am no muse—
Just hopelessly, painfully addicted
To kissing naked in the rain.

                    They get addicted.
         My love feels like their prescription.
                   I see it in their eyes—
          Unfolding like a movie in my mind,
               Each scene set to a symphony,
                          Escaping time.

Ripping silk dresses in hallways,
Held up by our breath.
Music in the stairwells—
A standing ovation at our finish.

If I could capture it in a scent,
I'd wear it daily, just for you.
Bottle it up, drench me in it.
Dress me down,
Or leave me in nothing but it.

I break their hearts
Because I'm afraid—
Afraid of the one thing they don't see:

I'm terrified of intimacy.

So I take off my clothes,
Do what I know best—
Seducing a man
Has always been my strength.

The problem is, I am the drug,
And they keep coming back for more.
I'm still waiting to find my cure.

So feed me.

Watch me.

Take my eyes, gasping on rooftops.
Fingers exploring,
Waxing pain to heat my body—
Candle flames, passionate rendezvous in public.

In the rain, I wore a white shirt
So you could see through.

I knew exactly what I was doing.

I knew exactly how to get you.

Get your fix, and watch me
Fill up your cup.
Tell me you want more.

Feed my ego.

Get higher and higher.
Love me,
Love me,
But don't
Say it.

Tennessee whisky

Don't sting like my fingers
In the cold, empty room—
Stuck in the chill
Of winter Nebraska.

I wanna feel
Ev-erything.
Somebody will find you—
That someone will be you.

Don't come back swinging
When you're blind to what's
In front of you.
But you ain't got knees
For the winter—
Your body will freeze up,
Stay still.

Looking out the window,
Thinking 'bout what could've been
While you could've taken
Your chance.

Tennessee whiskey—
Again.

You can blame everyone.
You can unload your gun.
You won't find any bones
In the closet.

Wear your life on
Your jacket,
Pockets ripped clean off.
Barely holding up,
Barely keeping you warm.

You're worn down now—
Battered, beaten.
Did you think it didn't matter?

Chase after your own dream.
Tennessee whiskey—
A double,
On number three.

I get drunk to stay warm—
To feel free.
It just got old—
Tennessee whiskey and me.

The life inside me
is bigger than the world
I see around me.

Speed dating for
ADHD

I get men so easily,
So quickly they fall in love with me.
I toss and turn,
Fearing the moment they make me choose—
One of them.

I want everyone,
Or no one at all.
But I don't want the heartache.

I love a man for five minutes,
Then I'm bored—
In love with the idea of love,
Not the process.

Sapio-*Sexual*

I live a dream life.
But the sunshine makes me sad.
I feel too many things all at once—
Or I don't feel a thing.

Forever never seems long enough,
But **NOW**
Doesn't come fast enough.
I'm restless.
For what?

I have a man in every city,
And a decorative place to sleep.
Yet I want more.

On my own, I seem broken.
Am I selfish?

I want a love that's all my own—
My Lower East Side rock star,
Without the addiction.

My Italian dream,
Without his handcuffs.

My passionate nights
With Mr. Puerto Rico,
But a commitment to healthy living—
Without sacrificing
My New York artist dream.

And all of them,
They want all of me.
I give, and I give,
Until there's nothing left for me.

When I say "no,"
Or "no thanks,"
I've changed—
I'm no fun.

Why?
Because I won't open my legs,
If you won't please me intellectually?

You won't pay me.
You don't see me.

Stimulating my senses
Takes more than this.

Open me up like a book.
Read me.
Take in my pages.
Study me,
And read between the lines.

Alcohol

I feel it dancing in the air.
She's coming up on my lungs,
My breathing's getting heavy.

Taste the blood in your glass,
Burnt your tongue.
You smack your gums,
Turning green.

Those lips keep moving—
I don't hear a thing.
The glitter in the air
Blinds my decisions.

When I drink her,
I lose my inhibitions.

From her breast,
I sank my teeth.
She's gonna ruin you—
Once she's had enough.

She regulates your mind
On a leash.
Declared her mine.

Little freaky.

~~You owe me money.~~

Fell in love
With everything he said,
Everything he did.

Have you ever,
just...

Fell for it?

All his stupid games,
Saying you weren't the same.

I'll tell you
How it hurts—
When he tells you
You ain't nothing
To him at all.

But you inspire an entire art collection.
The reason for his show.
The star of his success.

But, of course,
You mean nothing to him
At all.

Him.

He'll play dumb,
But deep down, he knows—
The gallery show,
The fashion line,
His change in clothes,
Taste in wine.

To him, the world is for stealing.
And you—the butterfly.
He needed your wings,
So he tried to steal them,
But couldn't manage the damage.

So, it must be you.
But you mean nothing.

The new perspective,
With me as the centerfold.
But, of course,
He came up with that art
On his own.

I can tell you how it feels—
Miserable inside.
Cause you're living a lie.
Living a lie.

You fall in love with art
Because you'll never have it.
(*At least not the talent.*)

~~Not for them.~~

Karma

If he only knew
That I was using you
To feel better
About me—
Better
About me, about you.

I know I'm not the only one
Who has used somebody
To get over somebody.

Maybe this is actually love.
Am I fooling myself
To get over himself?

Maybe I don't know who I am.
Or maybe I don't know
Who I was.

But I need somebody—
To get inside my body,
Read me like a map.
Discover what's ripping me open
From the inside out.

Taking me from me.
I'm dying to get out.

Let me in.
Set me free.
I'm using him
To learn more about me.

Smiling too much
Gets a girl in trouble.
Don't smile enough,
And you're still
Getting peddled.

Fruedian slip.

You don't really know me,
But you know all about me.
Got something that lingers

                        On my tongue—
                Come and taste it.
                    Take my breath,
                        Digest it.

I know you want it.
Watch me dancing.

            Take my clothes off with your eyes,
                        Fill me up,
            Watch me pour out in the night.

                    Moonlight mistress,
                        Latex dancer.
                Tonight on my knees—
                    Watch us moving.
                Make you make me
                            Free.

In the city, get busy—
The streets never bore me.
Private dancer,
Hopeless romancer.

King of thieves,
Stealing hearts from his sleeve.
But nobody seems to please me.

I dream of being taken,
Swept off my feet.
In real life, they're too sweet—
And I go crazy.

I want him to need it.

Obsessive.

I want him to hurt me.
I need him to need it.

Identiy
crisis.

Fever in a cage,
Holding the demons you've carried
Since a child.
Unmask the truth,
Let it all run wild.

Breaking out—
Nicotinamide death.
Tastes like the fear
Of leaving,
Addictive as crystal meth.

Letting go now—
Everything that once
Felt like home.

Fever rush.
Living in a cage.
Shoot the gun to your head—
Two choices:
Die awake,
Or walk among the dead.

Setting free the possibility
Of a new world.
Hold onto the fear,
Run for your life.

Run to the answers,
Run for a chance.
Push it down,
Falling down the throat
Of a smoking gun.

But don't react.
There's nowhere to turn,
Nowhere to go.

Pick up your head,
Fists to the sky.
No turning back,
Say your goodbyes.

Be gone.
Be dead.

Not yet

Remember that time it felt alright?
Can't remember the time I felt just right.
I just made excuses,
You told me things I always wanted to hear.

Tied me up—exotic.
Spun me 'round,
Slipped a pill—intoxicated.
We became two stars crashing down,
Ready to set the world on fire.

You burnt me to the ground
When I let your hands press against my neck.
Spinning since you kissed my lips,
I never found the ground.

I just wanted to be someone to somebody,
Wanted to be wanted—
Not just for my body.

But I always end up in the same place,
Crying on my bedroom floor.
Sometimes, I thought
I finally found the one—
Just desperately wanted to be loved by someone.

Falling apart because I need more.
I want love, any way I can get it,
But please, hurry up.
I don't think I can wait no more.

Men can be feminine.
Women can be masculine.
How we define those
Intricate finesses
Is what sets us apart.

You don't like me
Because I'm comfortable being ugly—
And that scares you.

A woman unafraid
To not be pretty.

Why won't you cry?
And when you do,
What for?

Why are you so afraid?
What eats you?

What do you stand for?

Stupid
people
disease.

Some of you are just fucking dumb.
There's this entire group of people
That really do suck that much.

And it sucks to suck.
Totally.

But I'd much rather know
What the fuck is going on—
And try to contribute.

It feels better existing
When you have bones.
Not the literal skeleton,
But substance.

There's weight in us.

Bitch
on
Heals.

I consider myself
A responsible delinquent.

Organized? Absolutely not.
But damn good
At looking hot.

Love
Is
ART

I love fashion
Because it's quick.
Instant results—
Wearing how I felt that day,
Expressing it

In textures, colors, and drapes.

It's art and armor.

Fashion can be a political statement.
Trends can change the world.
I guess it's all perspective.
Truly.

Expressing oneself is the point.
If I can't express my love
The way I express my clothes,
Am I truly making art—
Or just copying the scenery?

Art for oneself
Is a completely different feeling.
Masturbation, indeed.

And why not be so fuckable
You'd fuck yourself?

Art: expression with purpose for the world.
That's connection.

Designers design for others.
The buyer does it for themselves.
You see the point here?

Who cares.
Love shit.
Express it.

We gonna
talk
Or Fuck?

I'm too deep.
I can't linger just to let you feel safe
When I can't breathe.

I'm too intense—
The weight of my experience
Takes up space,
And I'm still working on it.

I'm too antisocial
To know how to stand
In this room of strangers.

Like they know something I don't.
Everyone's in on it but me.

I'm grooving,
But I'm probably gonna leave—
Cause mindless institutions
To numb your senses
Kill my brain.

I'd rather fall in love
In one evening
Than get drunk in a room
Of blank faces
That forget my name.

Death. Rebirth

I don't really know,
And I don't really care—
If this doesn't make me better,
Nothing ever will.

It's a jumpstart, baby.
When I hit the ground running,
I get up and go.

I'm so tired of the same routine—
Like I'm stuck in a loop.
If I jump off now,
I'd burn it all to the ground.

Something inside says
I have to keep going.
All of my insides are screaming,
Out of control.

I want to set fire
To the world—
And go.

Indigo nights

Your lips were never something
I meant to kiss,
But here you are—
In the middle of all of this.

Living life through a screen,
In a box where
Everyone can see.

There's nothing but a sheet
In between.
It doesn't bother me.

The most beautiful man I've seen
Stopped me dead in my tracks.
Do you see me?

Life on the inside
Doesn't bleed when you're weak.
It has us crawling.

Why can't I say my feelings?
At least give them some kind of meaning.
It's all just for show.
I don't really know—
But it's killing me.

He said,
"You don't have to feel needed
To be beautiful."

Why are you so kind?
Take my face in your hands,
Dive into my life.

Indigo nights,
Paint me in the sky.

It's hard letting go
Of something you've never had.
All alone.

He'll never know—

All my nights painted indigo.

If walls
could speak.

These walls wear like skin,
Sinking needles into your lies—
With permanent ink,
A tattoo of disguise.

"Mr. Perpetrator, predatory instigator,"
What's cooking in your mind?
You're licking up the dew,
What's left in the bottle—
Scraping for the very last high.

Give me that scratch, just to get that itch.
I don't wanna come calling out your name.

I've got a loaded gun in my pocket,
Stuffed with rose petals
And a carving of the date on your grave.

I want your sweet Monday cries,
That shivering pixie dust sigh.
Point the barrel between my eyes.
Pull the trigger on me, baby.
I know you want to—maybe.

Watch me bloom into ecstasy.
Watch me,
Watch me,
Watch me collapse into myself
Since your arms aren't there.

I press my ear to these walls,
And I can hear your heartbeat.
Fold yourself around me, within me.
Dance on the smoke from your loaded gun.

Trickle down this high.
What a feeling–
To feel these walls,
To sink into this high.

If these walls could speak,
They'd trade secrets of sisters past.
They'd taunt you,
Haunt you,
Call your name to the moon.

You wear these walls,
But they're all stained with your lies.

Bleed out,
Scream out,
Drown in a sea of tears.
These walls can't save you
If you're not really here.

Open me up,
Like your favorite book.

Indulge in me.

About the Author

Emily Carroo was born in the Windy City and still walks the streets of New York City, where she continues to set fire to its corners with art in all mediums. A perfumer since the age of four, she has graced stages across the United States with her many talents. For Emily, every day is a chance to express oneself. Writing fell into her lap after a string of notorious breakups and moments of extraordinary stupidity.

www.ingramcontent.com/pod-product-compliance
Lightning Source LLC
Chambersburg PA
CBHW040852120626
46547CB00006B/578